Contents

British Library Cataloguing in Publication Data

    All in a day.—(Poetry Series 831)
    1. English poetry
    I. Webb, Kaye
    821'.008   PR1175
    ISBN 0-7214-0850-8

First edition

© LADYBIRD BOOKS LTD MCMLXXXV

All in a day

Poems selected by Kaye Webb
illustrated by Kathie Layfield

Ladybird Books Loughborough

'I woke up
this morning'

Waking

My secret way of waking
is like a place
to hide.
I'm very still,
my eyes are shut.
They all think I am sleeping
but
I'm wide awake inside.

They all think I am sleeping
but
I'm wiggling my toes.
I feel sun-fingers
on my cheek.
I hear voices whisper-speak.
I squeeze my eyes
to keep them shut
so they will think I'm sleeping
BUT
I'm really wide awake inside
– and no one knows!

Lilian Moore

Morning jobs

From my bed I saw my clothes,
Empty and sad, and my shoes.
I'd drunk the milk out of my cup;
When morning comes I'll fill them up
I'll fill the cup with nice hot tea,
My clothes and shoes I'll fill with me.

Barbara Baker

Late for breakfast

*Who is it hides my sandals when I'm trying
to get dressed?
And takes away the hairbrush that was lying
on the chest?
I wanted to start breakfast before any of the
others
But something's always missing, or been
borrowed by my brothers.
I think I'd better dress at night, and eat my
breakfast too,
Then when everybody's hurrying –
I'll have nothing else to do.*

Mary Jeffries

Rain

I opened my eyes
And looked up at the rain
And it dripped in my head
And flowed into my brain
So pardon this wild crazy thing I just said
I'm just not the same since there's rain in my
                                           head.

I step very softly
I walk very slow
I can't do a hand-stand
Or I might overflow.
And all I can hear as I lie in my bed
Is the slishity-slosh of the rain in my head.

Shel Silverstein

Wide awake

I have to jump up
out of bed
and stretch my hands
and rub my head,
and curl my toes
and yawn
and shake
myself
all wide awake!

Myra Cohn Livingston

'Hullo, inside!'

Physical-education slides
Show us shots of our insides.
Every day I pat my skin,
'Thanks for keeping it all in.'

Max Fatchen

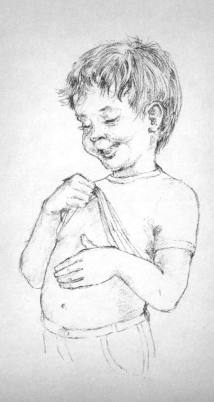

Baby's drinking song

As this poem is so short, it should be read at least three times
in quick succession, each time faster than the last.
Take a deep breath!

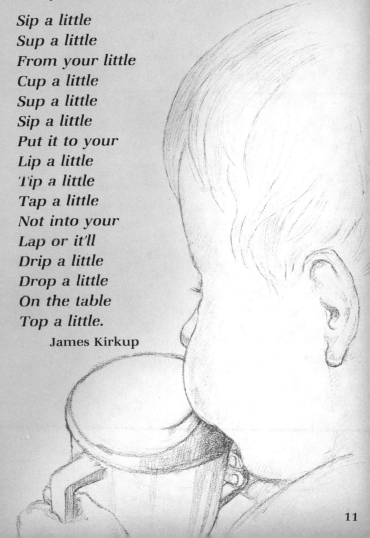

Sip a little
Sup a little
From your little
Cup a little
Sup a little
Sip a little
Put it to your
Lip a little
Tip a little
Tap a little
Not into your
Lap or it'll
Drip a little
Drop a little
On the table
Top a little.

James Kirkup

Egg thoughts

Soft-Boiled

I do not like the way you slide,
I do not like your soft inside,
I do not like you many ways,
And I could do for many days
Without a soft-boiled egg.

Sunny-Side-Up

With their yolks and whites all runny
They are looking at me funny.

Sunny-Side-Down

Lying face-down on the plate
On their stomachs there they wait.

Poached

Poached eggs on toast, why do you shiver
With such a funny little quiver?

Scrambled

I eat as well as I am able,
But some falls underneath the table.

Hard-Boiled

With so much suffering today
Why do them any other way?

Russell Hoban

A matter of taste

What does your tongue like the most?
Chewy meat or crunchy toast?

A lumpy bumpy pickle or tickly pop?
A soft marshmallow or a hard lime drop?

Hot pancakes or a sherbet freeze?
Celery noise or quiet cheese?

Or do you like pizza
More than any of these?

Eve Merriam

What you eat is what you get to be

Food is like
your clothes –
It dresses up
*   your bones!*

Mona Gould

The Pancake

Mix a pancake,
Stir a pancake,
Pop it in the pan.

Fry the pancake,
Toss the pancake,
Catch it if you can.

Christina Rossetti

Washing

What is all this washing about,
Every day, week in, week out?
From getting up till going to bed,
I'm tired of hearing the same thing said.
Whether I'm dirty or whether I'm not,
Whether the water is cold or hot,
Whether I like or whether I don't,
Whether I will or whether I won't, −
"Have you washed your hands and washed
    your face?"
I seem to live in the washing-place.

Whenever I go for a walk or ride,
As soon as I put my nose inside
The door again, there's someone there
With a sponge and soap, and a lot they care
If I have something better to do,
"Now wash your face and your fingers too."

Before a meal is ever begun,
And after ever a meal is done,
It's time to turn on the waterspout.

Please, what is all this washing about?

John Drinkwater

Yellow Poem

Each evening I eat lots of bread
with lots of yellow butter.
Enjoy my yellow omelette
with a little yellow cheese.

And before I make my yellow bed
in my tidy yellow room
I thank the Lord for yellowness
on my little yellow knees.

Roger McGough

(Q. Why were your knees yellow?
A. Because I'd been kneeling in custard.)

'School bell'

School is great

When I'm at home, I just can't wait
To get to school – I think it's great!

Assemblies I could do without,
But I love it, giving hymn-books out.

Writing's fun, when you try each letter,
But sharpening the pencils first – that's
better!

Football leaves me with the stitch,
But I'd miss my playtime to mark the pitch.

Cooking cakes gives you a thrill,
But cleaning the bowl out's better still.

Story's nice at the end of the day,
But I'd rather empty the rubbish away.

Yes, school's great – though I'll tell you what:
Going-home-time beats the lot!

Allan Ahlberg

School Bell

Nine-o'Clock Bell!
Nine-o'Clock Bell!
All the small children and big ones as well,
Pulling their stockings up, snatching their
hats,
Cheeking and grumbling and giving
back-chats,
Laughing and quarrelling, dropping their
things,
These at a snail's pace and those upon
wings,
Lagging behind a bit, running ahead,
Waiting at corners for lights to turn red,
Some of them scurrying,
Others not worrying,
Carelessly trudging or anxiously hurrying,
All through the streets they are coming
pell-mell
At the Nine-o'Clock
Nine-o'Clock
Nine-o'Clock
Bell!

Eleanor Farjeon

April Fool

The clock says ten,
You'll be late again –
Hurry and rush to school!

(The clock is right,
But it's ten at night –
Happy April Fool!)

Eve Merriam

In the playground

In the playground
Some run round
Chasing a ball
Or chasing each other;
Some pretend to be
Someone on TV;
Some walk
And talk,
Some stand
On their hands
Against the wall
And some do nothing at all.

Stanley Cook

Picking teams

When we pick teams in the playground,
Whatever the game might be,
There's always somebody left till last
And usually it's me.

I stand there looking hopeful
And tapping myself on the chest,
But the captains pick the others first,
Starting, of course, with the best.

Maybe if teams were sometimes picked
Starting with the worst,
Once in his life a boy like me
Could end up being first!

Allan Ahlberg

Supply Teacher

Here is the rule for what to do
Whenever your teacher has the flu,
Or for some other reason takes to her bed
And a different teacher comes instead.

When this visiting teacher hangs up her hat,
Writes the date on the board, does this or
that;
Always remember, you must say this:
'Our teacher never does that, Miss!'

When you want to change places or wander
about,
Or feel like getting the guinea-pig out,
Never forget, the message is this:
'Our teacher always lets us, Miss!'

Then, when your teacher returns next day
And complains about the paint or clay,
Remember these words, you just say this:
'That other teacher told us to, Miss!'

Allan Ahlberg

'Things that run and swim and fly'

Mick

Mick my mongrel-O
Lives in a bungalow,
Painted green with a round doorway.
With an eye for cats
And a nose for rats
He lies on his threshold half the day.
He buries his bones
By the rockery stones,
And never, oh never, forgets the place.
Ragged and thin
From his tail to his chin,
He looks at you with a sideways face.
Dusty and brownish,
Wicked and clownish,
He'll win no prize at the County Show.
But throw him a stick,
And up jumps Mick,
And right through the flower-beds see him go!

James Reeves

Wishing

If I could have
Any wish that could be

I'd wish that a dog
Could have me.

Eve Merriam

My brother

Today I went to market with my mother.
I always help her buy the things we eat.
Not sitting in the pushcart like my brother
Who gets our dinner piled around his feet.
I know where jam is. Coffee. Bread and
                                    butter.
Each thing I bring she says to Davy: "No!
Don't touch that, Sweetie!" Mostly Davy
                                    doesn't.
This morning Davy did some touching
                                    though –
He spread his hair with cottage cheese all
                                    over.
Bit through the paper. Gave our ham a
                                    chew.
Liked the butter. "Davy!" cried my mother.
She started in to scold my little brother.
Couldn't.
Burst out laughing.
I did too.

                                    Dorothy Aldis

The Pet

I asked my mum
If I could have a pet
'One day' she said,
'But not yet. Not yet.'

I was five then
And each year I tried
'Not yet, not yet'
Mum always replied

I'm ten now
And big for my age
And I've just built
A wooden cage

For now I've a pet
To put inside
Something belonging
To someone who died

He keeps me company
When I feel sad
He's my pet slipper
And I call him 'Dad'.

Roger McGough

Friends

I fear it's very wrong of me
And yet I must admit,
When someone offers friendship
I want the whole of it.
I don't want everybody else
To share my friends with me.
At least, I want one special one,
Who indisputedly,

Likes me much more than all the rest,
Who's always on my side,
Who never cares what others say,
Who lets me come and hide
Within his shadow, in his house –
It doesn't matter where –
Who lets me simply be myself,
Who's always, always there.

Elizabeth Jennings

Jump or jiggle

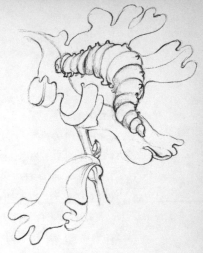

Frogs jump
Caterpillars hump

Worms wiggle
Bugs jiggle

Rabbits hop
Horses clop

Snakes slide
Sea-gulls glide

Mice creep
Deer leap

Puppies bounce
Kittens pounce

Lions stalk —
But —
I walk!

      Evelyn Beyer

Pet Shop

At our pet shop you can buy
Things that run and swim and fly,
But never once have I seen them sell,
Anything as big as an el-
ephant or albatross,
Crocodile, bear, rhinoceros,
Nor ever a creature as small, alas,
As a kingfisher, or grass-
hopper, earwig, bumble-bee,
Minnow, mole, or common flea,
O, I really think it is absurd
They don't keep a whale or a ladybird.

Leonard Clark

The Abominable Snowman

I've never seen an abominable snowman,
I'm hoping not to see one,
I'm also hoping, if I do,
That it will be a wee one.

Ogden Nash

'Time to go home'

Time to go home

Time to go home!
  Says the great steeple clock.
Time to go home!
  Says the gold weathercock.
Down sinks the sun
  In the valley to sleep;
Lost are the orchards
  In blue shadows deep.
Soft falls the dew
  On cornfield and grass;
Through the dark trees
  The evening airs pass:
Time to go home,
  They murmur and say;
Birds to their homes
  Have all flown away.
Nothing shines now
  But the gold weathercock.
Time to go home!
  Says the great steeple clock.

James Reeves

Bedtime

Five minutes, five minutes more, please!
  Let me stay five minutes more!
Can't I just finish the castle
  I'm building here on the floor?
Can't I just finish the story
  I'm reading here in my book?
Can't I just finish this bead-chain —
  It almost is finished, look!
Can't I just finish this game, please?
  When a game's once begun
It's a pity never to find out
  Whether you've lost or won.
Can't I just stay five minutes?
  Well, can't I stay just four?
Three minutes, then? two minutes?
  Can't I stay one minute more?

Eleanor Farjeon

It's a bit rich

Playing Monopoly's
Really my scene.
I hang on to houses
And play very mean.

I take all the money.
There's often a stack.
I'm not very pleasant
When giving it back.

I'm harsh as a landlord.
I've nothing for sale.
I'm buying your station.
You're going to jail.

My fistful of money –
It seems such a shame
When bedtime arrives
And it's only a game.

Max Fatchen

Before the bath

It's cold, cold, cold,
And the water shines wet,
And the longer I wait
The colder I get.

I can't quite make
Myself hop in
All shivery-cold
In just my skin.

Yet the water's warm
In the tub, I know.
So — one, two, three,
And IN I go!

Corinna Marsh

After a bath

After my bath
I try, try, try
to wipe myself
till I'm dry, dry, dry.

Hands to wipe
and fingers and toes
and two wet legs
and a shiny nose.

Just think how much
less time I'd take
if I were a dog
and could shake, shake, shake.

Aileen Fisher

39

'Dreams to sell'

If there were dreams to sell,
    What would you buy?
Some cost a passing bell;
    Some a light sigh,
That shakes from Life's fresh crown
Only a roseleaf down.
If there were dreams to sell,
Merry and sad to tell,
And the crier rung the bell,
    What would you buy?

                Thomas Lovell Beddoes

I'm alone in the evening

I'm alone in the evening
when the family sits
reading and sleeping,
and I watch the fire in close
to see flame goblins
wriggling out of their caves
for the evening

Later I'm alone
when the bath has gone cold around me
and I have put my foot
beneath the cold tap
where it can dribble
through valleys between my toes
out across the white plain of my foot
and bibble bibble into the sea

I'm alone
when mum's switched out the light
my head against the pillow
listening to ca-thump ca-thump
in the middle of my ears.
It's my heart.

Michael Rosen

Counting sheep

They said
'If you can't get to sleep
    try counting sheep.'
I tried.
It didn't work.

They said,
'Still awake! Count rabbits, dogs,
    or leaping frogs!'
I tried.
It didn't work.

They said,
'It's very late! Count rats,
    or red-eyed bats!'
I tried.
It didn't work.

They said,
'Stop counting stupid sheep!
    EYES CLOSED! DON'T PEEP!'
I tried
and fell asleep.

                          Wes Magee

Good Night

Now good night.
Fold up your clothes
As you were taught,
Fold your two hands,
Fold up your thought;
Day is the plough-land,
Night is the stream,
Day is for doing
And night is for dream.
Now good night.

Eleanor Farjeon

43

Acknowledgments

*The compiler and publishers would like to thank the following
for permission to use copyright poems in this anthology.*

Eleanor Farjeon's School Bell *taken from* Collected Poems and
reprinted by permission of Oxford University Press and the author;
Eleanor Farjeon's Bedtime *taken from* Silver, Sand and Snow *and*
Good Night *taken from* Quartet of Poets, *reprinted by permission
of* Michael Joseph *and the author;* Russell Hoban's Egg thoughts
taken from Egg thoughts and other Frances Songs *and reprinted
by permission of* Faber and the author; *Wes Magee's* Counting sheep
reprinted by permission of the author © Wes Magee *and taken from*
All the Day Through *published by Bell and Hyman Ltd;* James Reeves'
Mick and Time to go home *taken from* The Wandering Moon *and
reprinted by permission of* William Heinemann Limited; *Roger McGough's*
Yellow Poem *and* The Pet *taken from* Sky in the Pie *published by
Kestrel Books Ltd and reprinted by permission of A D Peters and Co Ltd;*
Aileen Fisher's After a bath *taken from* Up the Windy Hill *published by
Abelard Press, New York 1953. Copyright renewed 1981 and reprinted
by permission of the author;* James Kirkup's Baby's drinking song *taken
from* White Shadows, Black Shadows *published by J M Dent and Sons Ltd
and reprinted by permission of the author;* Mary Jeffries' Late for breakfast
taken from Allsorts *published by* Methuen Children's Books Ltd *and
reprinted by permission of the author;* Shel Silverstein's Rain *taken from*
Where the Sidewalk Ends: The Poems and Drawings of Shel Silverstein.
Copyright © 1974 *by Snake Eye Music Inc reprinted by permission of*
Harper and Row, Publishers, Inc; My brother *by Dorothy Aldis reprinted
by permission of* G P Putnam's Sons *from* Hop, Skip and Jump!
Copyright 1934. Copyright renewed © 1961 *by Dorothy Aldis;* Mona Gould's
What you eat is what you get to be *taken from* Round Slice of the Moon
published by Scholastic-TAB Publications Ltd *and reprinted by permission of
the author;* Myra Cohn Livingston's Wide awake *taken from* Wide Awake
and other Poems *by Myra Cohn Livingston* © 1959 *by Myra Cohn Livingston
and reprinted by permission of Marian Reiner for the author;*
Elizabeth Jennings' Friends *taken from* As Large as Alone *published by
Macmillan and reprinted by permission of Macmillan and the author;*
Hullo, inside *and* It's a bit rich *by Max Fatchen from* Max Fatchen:
Wry Rhymes for Troublesome Times *(Kestrel Books 1983) pp 55, 78.
Copyright* © 1983 *by Max Fatchen and reprinted by permission
of Penguin Books Ltd;* School is great, Picking teams *and*
Supply Teacher *by Allan Ahlberg from* Allan Ahlberg: Please Mrs Butler
(Kestrel Books 1983) pp 17, 35, 80. Copyright © 1983 *by Allan Ahlberg
and reprinted by permission of Penguin Books Ltd;*